CRISIS STATES

BEFORE YOU START TO READ THIS BOOK, take this moment to think about making a donation to punctum books, an independent non-profit press,

@ https://punctumbooks.com/support/

If you're reading the e-book, you can click on the image below to go directly to our donations site. Any amount, no matter the size, is appreciated and will help us to keep our ship of fools afloat. Contributions from dedicated readers will also help us to keep our commons open and to cultivate new work that can't find a welcoming port elsewhere. Our adventure is not possible without your support.
Vive la open-access.

Fig. 1. Hieronymus Bosch, *Ship of Fools* (1490–1500)

First published in 2016 by punctum books, Earth, Milky Way.
www.punctumbooks.com

ISBN-13: 978-0988234086
ISBN-10: 0988234084
Library of Congress Cataloging Data is available from the Library of Congress

Book design: Vincent W.J. van Gerven Oei

Jeff Shantz

CRISIS STATES

Governance, Resistance
& Precarious Capitalism

Ⓟ

CONTENTS

THE STATE OF
CRISIS TODAY

I F WE COULD USE BUT one word to define the current period, that word would have to be *crisis*. From the economic crisis that has wrecked the lives of millions, to the political crisis wracking liberal democracies, to the crisis of confidence undermining peoples' hopes, to the ecological crisis threatening life itself on planet Earth, through to the crisis of legitimacy impacting all of these, *crisis* is the watchword of the day. It is not wrong to suggest that we are living in a state of crisis. Other terms that speak to the tenor of the times include *austerity, precarity, neoliberalism, insecurity,* and *risk*. And these are closely linked to, and contribute to, the oppressive climate of crisis. They give flesh to the all-pervasive sense of crisis.

This state of crisis takes on the multiple forms of economic restructuring (layoffs, flexibilization, just-in-time production, workplace closures and withdrawals, insecurity and precarization of labor) and social restructuring (cuts to social services, withdrawal of social welfare, privatization of public resources, social scarcity, and austerity policies) to satisfy corporate owners, bankers, and investors. These are accompanied by and facilitated through political crises — not the least of which are the "no alternative-ism" of the electoral framework (of the two-sided single partyism of Republicrats in the US) and the "too big to fail" squeamishness in the face of corporate arrogance and malfeasance. All while militarizing police (who kill with impunity), legislatively punishing "bad thoughts," securitizing borders, and pursuing the moral panic-based phobias of war on terror campaigns. And all of which is underwritten by environmental crises associated with extreme energy and extractives industries — and the wars and conflicts related to these. (While these are deeply internal in the impacts on human life they are mythically externalized in dominant political and economic worldviews.)

The crises of our time take on the character, as social commentator Alain Badiou suggests, of a "law of the world," at least for our masters (2012, 4). Yet, despite the sense, manufactured in mainstream economic, political, and media discourses, that crisis is something inexplicable or unstoppable, beyond human control, these crises all have roots in specific social actions, policies, practices, and visions. They are all part of, and contribute to, broader social struggles playing out over the course of decades. They have specific origins and in many ways specific intentions. They emerge from and contribute to — they constitute — shifting terrains of social conflict and control, struggles over resources and over responsibilities. They hold in the balance the future of human care and welfare. Their outcomes will determine the character of human sociality and interaction.

The state has always been the instrument *par excellence* for manufacturing social crisis. This is done at base through the production of death — which is what the history of states is really all about. But the state has other ways of manufacturing crisis. One is through the construction of scarcity (which states have also always been about at base). Others include the inferiorization, and separation, of peoples. These often go hand in hand (scarcity as a constructed condition of the inferiorized who may, in fact, have been involved in the actual production of surplus). A fundamental process (and goal) of states is categorization and division of the population, particularly the attempt to divide the population between normal and deviant (and thus suspect). The state can be defined as an institution for imposing norms on a whole population (Badiou 2012, 92). And in the current period those norms are norms of crisis and precariousness.

The tools at the state's disposal are well known. Police violence, denial of documents, refusal of services, the infamous cuts to necessary resources, detention and restraints on mobility, etc. The punishing of "bad thoughts." Surveillance and moral regulation. Telling women what they can and cannot wear.

As we will see, the sense that we are living in a state of crisis has a dual meaning. On the one hand crisis marks our conditions of life, of interrelation, of collective and individual feeling. At the same time it is also true, if less sensed and certainly less remarked upon, that the multiple crises of our age have very real roots in specific forms of state organization of social life, state policies and practices. And these Crisis States shape human life and interaction in ways that further relate to processes of accumulation and exploitation (which further states of crisis and Crisis States).

The crisis has been effected through, and toward, destruction of the shared, collective resources of working class struggle built up over decades. This includes destruction or diminishment of what I call working class infrastructures of resistance (unions, community centers, political groups, etc.) (Shantz 2010). It also occurs through the discrediting of ideas that oppose fully the ideologies of state capital — most notably anarchism, socialism, communism, but also anti-colonial and anti-racist expressions.

Badiou wryly boils down the social and political crisis of our times to the actions of a tiny oligarchy — a clique of gangsters (2012, 12–13). In his biting terms the crisis amounts to thuggish commands of the mafia of capital, before which governments of all stripes genuflect and tremble. These commands are of this quality:

> "Privatize everything. Abolish help for the weak, the solitary, the sick and the unemployed. Abolish all aid for everyone except the banks. Don't look after the poor; let the elderly die. Reduce the wages of the poor, but reduce the taxes of the rich. Make everyone work until they are ninety. Only teach mathematics to traders, reading to big property-owners and history to on-duty ideologues." And the execution of these commands will in fact ruin the life of millions of people. (2012, 13)

For some seeking an explanation for the crisis, there has emerged a notion of "postmodern capitalism." This is a capitalism of global scope and scale that supposedly bypasses or sheds the power of the state. This is supposedly, too, a capitalism of novelty. Yet a proper examination shows that this capitalism replays much of earlier forms of capitalist development and does so, as ever before, through specific (but always, in various forms, engaged and present) deployments of the state. Without the state no capitalism or its market has ever been possible. So too today. As Alain Badiou points out, what is the much ballyhooed "globalization" but the "world market" discussed over 150 years ago by Marx? For Badiou, "Basically, today's world is exactly the one which, in a brilliant anticipation, a kind of true science fiction, Marx heralded as the full unfolding of the irrational and, in truth, monstrous potentialities of capitalism" (2012, 12). Badiou suggests that we are even now already in a period beyond crisis and well into the period of barbarism against which Marx saw communism as the only hope.

In the manufacture of crisis through social means the state is restored in its role, as Marx called it, of the executive of the bourgeoisie. In saying this it is important to clarify that it is not geared to specific outcomes for specific players (this or that capitalist, Wal-Mart over Target say) in the manner of instrumental conspiracy. Rather it is geared toward conditions most conducive to accumulation and exploitation (profitability) for capital generally.

The generalization, or socialization, of crisis renders labor desperate and dependent. It makes all of the working class susceptible to labor under the least satisfactory conditions. It asserts the coercive character of the labor market in a context of no alternatives. If one wants to survive one will work under whatever conditions are presented. One will not hold out for, or dare ask for, better. This is the social impact of generalized, of socialized, precarity.

Power, according to theorist of bare life Giorgio Agamben, "no longer has today any form of legitimization other than emergency" (2000, 6). Power "everywhere and continuously refers and appeals to emergency as well as laboring secretly to produce it" (Agamben 2000, 6). As Agamben asks, "How could we not think that a system that can no longer function at all except on the basis of emergency would not also be interested in preserving such an emergency at any price" (2000, 6). This is life reduced to bare life, precarious, threatened. And state practice in its expanding drive for austerity for all but the elites is willing to go to extremes of violence and brutality.

For those most harmed by the crisis and for those who attempt to oppose it (not always the same) the state has reserved particularly violent, indeed brutal, treatment. From blanket policing of poor neighborhoods (under tough-on-crime "broken windows" ideology to mass incarceration to extrajudicial violence, and outright public executions, by police) the recent period has seen an all-out assault on poor and racialized neighborhoods, on communities of the precarious.

The tenor of the times, its open, unapologetic, bald-faced exertion of state violence and the courage of opposition from among the subjugated, is perhaps most forcefully expressed in the Ferguson rebellion following the police killing of Mike Brown and in the rebellions and uprisings that have emerged since, especially after the public and recorded execution by police of Eric Garner in New York, which have converged around the #BlackLivesMatter banner. The numerous killings of unarmed and non-threatening black people (men, women, trans), which have received necessary popular scrutiny and response, show the base character of a Crisis State, one poised and prepared to kill without explanation, to bring crisis to poor, marginalized working class individuals and communities. At the same time, the brave, clearsighted, unflinching opposition, often bare but always honest in its expression and warm in its care and solidarity, provides one of the most inspiring, promising, and profound examples of a new resistance. The movements have truly transformed understandings and expectations of politics in the face of what can only be described as terrifying violence and the very real, immediate presence of conscienceless state lethality. In the face of a murderous state they present an emerging constructive commons.

Alain Badiou, in reflecting on the present time of riots, sees the current period as similar to the period following 1848 in Europe. It is a period of resurgent liberatory forces of the subjected. Like 1848, a period of reawakening emerges from a period of "end of history" ruling class triumphalism and reaction.

If we are in a period of state capitalist barbarism, and the crises of our times provide ample evidence that we are, then we might well ask where the way out of crisis opens. What is being posed as the equivalent in the counter to barbarism previously located in socialism?

The mobilizations of this decade have taken the form of uprisings against subjugation and have shown a willingness (at times even a commitment) to operate outside the limiting bounds of legality or lawfulness. From black bloc organizing during alternative globalization demonstrations around various issues to the #BlackLivesMatter movements initiated in response to police executions of community members, there has been a reinvigoration of politics emphasizing autonomy, a self-valorizing impetus that is not restricted within statist confines of the political. The uprisings assert self care and social welfare beyond the demands of the state and legal or peaceful protest, on state terms. They also raise demands and propose organizing practices that go beyond reformist appeals of traditional statist and electoral politics.

The new risings are not only renovating or innovating politics with their tenor and tone, strategies and tactics, and scope of vision. They are also innovating modes of organizing. Today's movements organize in ways that are decentralized, horizontal, nonhierarchical, participatory, and anti-authoritarian. They are typically autonomous, not tied to specific parties or political structures, and self-directed rather than run by central bodies, boards, or executives. They are agile and expansive.

In Western liberal democracies the new movements against crisis assert the self-identifying, self-determining open post-citizenship belonging of "no one is illegal" and anti-borders movements, the anti-colonial sovereignty of Idle No More and indigenous uprisings, the unapologetic, self-valorizing actions of new poor people's movements, the defiance of property regimes in rent strikes and foreclosure resistance, the sabotage of ecojustice and deep green movements, the assertive alternatives of anarchism, and more. All of these offer new proposals for politics. They have each suggested new infrastructures for resistance. While still in early forms of development, these new eruptions have in many startling and exciting ways, within a period of crisis, brought the institutions and organizations of economic and political power, states and capital, to their own crisis. And this suggests an opening in the politics of resistance and social transformation that is shifting the terrain of political struggle in ways that have not been seen in decades within liberal democratic contexts.

STATE AND CAPITAL: FROM PLANNER STATE TO CRISIS STATE

DESPITE MAINSTREAM DISCOURSES THAT ATTEMPT to pose a dichotomy or opposition between the state and capital or the so-called free market (free with regard to state interference if nothing else), the capitalist market has never developed, indeed could not develop, without the active support and reinforcement of the state. On the one hand, the market has depended fundamentally on state force to dispossess, i.e. steal, lands and resources from local populations, to displace local populations who want their lands and resources back, and to impose a desperation and dependency on people such that they are coerced into selling their labor to capital, on the infamous labor market, in order to survive. Such is the history of capitalist development since, at least, the enclosures. On the other hand, capital has required the state to impose its ownership rights, through legislation and force, its conditions of exploitation of labor, its private control over the products of collective labor, and so forth. At the same time the state has been required to establish moral rules by which the exploited and disposed accept, if grudgingly, the rules of the game, conditions of work, the "naturalness" of inequality, etc. This includes prohibitions on theft and self-redistribution of resources as well as moral invocations to accept one's lot in life and not rebel (beyond limited legalistic forms of protest). Simply put, without the state the exploited and oppressed would neither accept their exploitation and oppression, nor would they limit their opposition to means and ends dictated by economic and political powerholders.

All of this and more are essential to maintaining conditions of resource distribution, exploitation, and accumulation under capitalist social relations. And these tasks have been delegated largely to states rather than taken on as the private (and costly) endeavors of capital and the market. As Alisa Del Re notes:

> The State is the institution that historically has regulated the adjustment between the process of accumulation and the process of social reproduction of the population. Modern States control the conflicts inherent to the distribution of waged labor, the specific distribution of labor, and the resources that it entails. (Del Re 1996, 102)

An associated concern is also the reproduction of the working class itself. Typically the care and reproduction of the working class has been privatized (within the nuclear family form itself) and the costs of restoring the current generation of workers and producing the next generations borne by the working class itself. This has been accompanied by various rebellions and resistance as this cost has been negotiated or refused or repayment (from capital) has been sought. Social movements of the mid-twentieth century were often oriented around these issues of reproduction (education, health care, housing, environment, etc.).

A workable balance between these processes, managed by the state, "represents the condition for the continuity of the process of capitalist accumulation" (Del Re 1996, 102). As autonomist Marxist theorist Nick Dyer-Witheford (1999) notes, capital has increasingly been unwilling and unable to take the reproductive activity of the proletariat for granted. In his view, "To ensure the proper supply and disciplining of the minds and bodies required for work, it has been compelled to extend systematically its control over society as a whole a control mediated through the Leviathan-like structures of the state" (Dyer-Witheford 1999, 100–101). And this occurs through, and in the context of, social struggles over the distribution and control of collective resources.

And the mask of democracy should not obscure these social relationships. Democracy is really, as Badiou suggests, merely the name given to a state system particularly suited to the peaceful coexistence of the factions that make up the ruling oligarchy on general terms of agreement (market economy, parliamentarism, anti-communism/hatred of alternatives) (2012, 28). Current struggles open up alternative, horizontal, participatory notions of democracy and impel rethinking of democratic practice. At the same time there are strong forces, including from within the Left itself, within the opposition, that strive to restrain opposition within parliamentary "democratic" forms (the worn-out forms of social democracy persist in forms like the New Democratic Party in Canada or Syriza in Greece).

On the Planner State

In the first half of the twentieth century, the threat of militant working-class movements pushed advanced capitalist societies to shift from a Rights State, in which government activity was limited largely to securing the conditions for the free market, to a Planner State, or the social citizenship state (Dyer-Witheford 1999). The Planner State arrangements include the various welfare state provisions often designated as Keynesianism or social democracy.

The Planner State emerges in response to, and always as part of, the question of administration of labor and the need of capital, as much as possible, to manage accumulation. Particularly, it addresses a period of unrest and instability (depression, war, reconstruction) and the presence of an alternative, or perceived alternative (however imperfect). The social management of accumulation and reproduction, and of production relations within processes of value extraction or exploitation, has also been encapsulated within the notion of Fordism (mass production and labor peace and mass provisions of social services). The conditions of the Planner State tie labor "peace" and productive stability, in growth, to a redeployment of surplus value into social mechanisms of reproduction (of the working class, for sure, but of class relations more broadly). Fordist arrangements.

Under the Planner State the reproduction of labor power was managed by the state through the institutional networks of schools, hospitals, welfare programs and unemployment provisions (Dyer-Witheford 1999). This is generally referred to as the welfare state. Movements in response to the "insecurity of access to the means of survival for citizens" pushed the state to assume expanded responsibilities for the population (Del Re 1996, 102). These structures of welfare under Fordist relations were based on the logic of "the reproduction of the norm of the wage relationship" (Vercellone 1996, 84). All of this occurred within mass productivist frameworks. As Dyer-Witheford notes, "For the schools, health care systems, and various forms of social payments of the Planner State cultivated the increasingly healthy, educated, and peaceful forms of 'human capital' necessary for intensive technoscientific development of the Fordist era" (Dyer-Witheford 1999, 101). Entry into the realm of the secured was predicated on participation in processes of growth.

Welfare state provisions, such as social assistance, social security, and public health, "represent a form of income and social services distribution" (Del Re 1996, 101). Part of this is a crucial shift from the sphere of production to the sphere of reproduction "where what is guaranteed and controlled (without direct links to production but nonetheless aimed at it) is the reproduction of individuals" (Del Re 1996, 101). And reproduced in specific ways.

But what emerges is, as many anarchists have pointed out, the expansion of the state into ever-growing realms of social life. From consumption practices, to leisure activities, to school attendance, to personal hygiene, or public nudity, that state asserts routines and regimes of normalization (and deviance).

The social citizenship, or Planner State, "administratively distributes legality so as to reintegrate the underprivileged classes within the fiction of a guaranteed community in exchange for renouncing the virtual subversiveness of difference" (Illuminati 1996, 176). That deal also imposed specific rules of action and regulated oppositional activity within specific legal and moral frameworks. Thus the Planner State was accompanied by various moral panics and the policing of deviance among the working class and poor.

The Planner State crystallized the biopolitical character of state capitalist development. The health and wealth of the state depended clearly and increasingly on the health of the population (Lorey 2015, 25). The strength of the bourgeois state depends on the "happiness" of the population (which emerges as a population for its own sake) (Lorey 2015, 24). As Del Re puts it, "The Welfare State is established once the secular principle of solidarity is substituted for the religious principle of solidarity. The idea is that all citizens have the right to live decently, even when the events of their lives, starting from unfavorable initial chances, would not allow it" (1996, 101). But this was never equally or evenly distributed and was founded on the precarity of specific sections of the population against whom protection was sought.

The Planner State never overcame or ended precarity, nor was it ever designed to do so. It was, rather, geared toward management of precarity (largely in a way that would fend off insurrection). The threat of precarity served to gain the obedience of the industrial working classes throughout the period of the Planner State arrangements.

Growing the State, Growing Crisis:
On the Crisis State

The vast social struggles of the 1960s and 1970s, including the struggles of the new social movements, began to corrode the basis of the Planner State. As autonomist Marxist theorist Dyer-Witheford suggests, "Movements of workers, the unemployed, welfare recipients, students and minority groups began to make demands on the vast system of social administration that transgressed the limits set by capitalist logic" (1999, 101). In a very real sense the concerns with life and welfare, which had formed the working class side of the historic post-war compromise, came up against the demands of capital for intensified accumulation and exploitation (which outstripped the gains afforded by the promise of labor peace which rank-and-file movements increasingly refused by the mid-1970s).

The growing demands of communities and movements posed costs too great for capital from the perspective of profitability. Even more troubling for capital were the demands crystallizing within certain sectors of the working classes for control of the economy and social production itself. These were expressed in dramatic forms in the general strikes in France in 1968 and Quebec in 1972, but also in more quotidian terms in growing strike waves throughout the decade from 1965 to 1975. Within formal channels the assertions of the working classes were expressed in demands for increases in welfare state provisions, and areas of coverage as well. As Dyer-Witheford puts it:

> These encroachments were intolerable for North American and European capital, whose rate of profit was already being squeezed by shop-floor militancy and international competition. Its response part of the larger neoliberal restructuring offensive was to repudiate the postwar social contract and dismantle the Planner State, destroying what it could no longer control. (1999, 101)

The move to dismantle the Planner State arrangements and break up the welfare state provisions is carried out within the framework given the now infamous name of neoliberalism. Its *modus operandi* is austerity, and its impacts are the growth of poverty and spread of homelessness as national crises along with the growing wealth gap and the disparity between rich and poor. More recently some have worried over the decline of the middle class, which is really a misnaming of the growing precarity and insecurity of the working class.

The state form advancing through the neoliberal policies effects a social organization of crisis. As Dyer-Witheford states it, "In the realm of government, the Planner State is replaced by the 'Crisis State' — a regime of control by trauma" (1999, 76). This trauma is expressed in the now-familiar forms of austerity, precarity, social service cuts, growing economic inequality, poverty, homelessness, militarized policing, criminalization of dissent, etc. Under the Crisis State, the state governs fundamentally by planning or, more commonly, simply allowing crises within the subordinate classes.

This reflects, significantly, evolving efforts by capital to re-arrange relations of production and re-engineer the organization of labor towards increased profitability (and restored control over the labor process). The Crisis State emerges as part of shifting forms of accumulation, notably the projects of capitalist globalization,

> in which certain sectors throughout the world, capital is moving away from dependence on large-scale industries toward new forms of production that involve more immaterial and cybernetic forms of labor, flexible and precarious networks of employment, and commodities increasingly defined in terms of culture and media. (Hardt 1996, 4)

This is what is perhaps too often called "the postmodernization of production." These new forms of production (flexibilization, precarious work, just-in-time production, computerization, boutique economies, networked production) marked a radical break from the Fordist arrangement of mass concentrations of labor power (of secure work in large-scale workplaces and centralized production forms).

Dyer-Witheford suggests that the post Fordist phase, in which the Fordist organization of the social factory is dismantled, "must be understood as a technological and political offensive aimed at decomposing social insubordination" (1999, 76).

The technological has been effected through work restructuring (flexibilization, just-in-time production, globalization and capital strike, precarization of work) in pursuit of new forms of accumulation. These are the shifts represented in deindustrialization and high-tech new economies, for example (the computerization of workplaces allowed for increased profitability and exploitation but also ensured so-called downsizing, temporary employment, union busting, etc.). The political represents the most dramatic and disturbing forms of the Crisis States, from law and order policing and the "war on drugs" to mass incarceration (all directed overwhelmingly against dissident racialized communities) to the violence of homelessness and the attacks on the poor and homeless pursued under the rubric of "broken windows" crime policies. We might include here too the criminalization of dissent and punishment of oppositional political movements.

The social impacts are dire. And they are intended to be. The reactionary articulation posed by Thatcher in England, Reagan in the US and Mulroney in Canada asserted a repudiation of the social itself. Thatcher openly proclaimed, "There is no society." And Crisis State actions have been in large part directed toward the dismantling of social resources of value to the majority of society's members (but which are viewed as costly burdens by capital and by state actors alike). As Dyer-Witheford notes:

> On the one hand, privatization, deregulation, and cutbacks systematically subvert the welfare state, slashing the social wage, weeding out enclaves of popular control, and attacking any of labour's protections from the disciplinary force of the market. The costs of reproducing labour power increasingly devolve back onto individuals and households. This shift becomes ever more important to capital as corporate downsizing and automation ejects more and more workers from production, thereby swelling the ranks of the unemployed and impoverished, increasing welfare roles and diminishing tax revenues. (1999, 101)

These create conditions for intensified accumulation of capital, through reorganization of work, re-assertion of ownership and management claims of capital, and the dependency of people on the labor market, without social alternatives in welfare state provisions. At the same time social resources themselves become privatized, turned into mechanisms of value extraction and profitability. And in Thatcherite fashion, society is rendered obsolete and all that remains is the individual and the family. As a rather painful expression of this we might also recall the numerous neoliberal ideologues who blame poverty, criminalization, mass incarceration, addiction, and violence in poor neighborhoods on a "breakdown of the family" (see Elder 2001; 2012; Moynihan 1986; Wilson 1993; 1997; 2010).

The agenda of cuts under neoliberal regimes of austerity have given rise to a line of theorizing which proposes a lean state reduced in size, function, and funding. Rather than the "lean state" we are better served by the autonomist Marxists' discussions of the crisis state. The lean state designation suggests that the state has shrunk or is somehow more passive than in the past. Lean state also implies that the state would be used for purposes of social and personal support if only it had the resources, if only it were robust rather than lean. All of these depictions are inaccurate. The lean state is in fact an enlarged activist state with no interest in providing for human needs or security. The crisis state designation captures the real spirit of the contemporary state as one which intervenes regularly to bring large segments of the population to crisis.

Yet the well-known cuts of Crisis State austerity are only part of the equation of effecting broad social crisis. As Dyer-Witheford (1999) notes, the new regime of governance under the Crisis State has a dual character, of which analyses of the Lean State capture only one side.

Yet the other side of Crisis State transformations has been as prevalent and as significant for capital. This is the massive build-up, and associated public funding expenditures, of the openly repressive apparatuses. Not all state programs are viewed alike for the cuts advocates. As Dyer-Witheford notes, "On the other hand, those aspects of the state necessary to the protection of accumulation such as the security apparatus or subsidization of high-technology investment are strengthened" (1999, 101–102). The agenda of cutbacks is the side of the Crisis State that theorists of the lean state have tended to focus on but this has meant, as is too often assumed, that the state is being reduced. Rather, cuts in one area, social provision, has been a growth in the repressive functions.

The neoliberal claim of a shrunken state, the favored trope of Republicans since Reagan, is revealed as a chimera. While Republican ideology uses a phony commitment to reduced government, behind a populist appeal to cut spending or get the bureaucrats off people's backs, the reality is that neoliberal governments, from Reagan on, have actually increased government spending and scope. But they have done so in very particular ways suited to the new regime of accumulation and regulation.

One can see from the start the activist characteristics of Crisis State policies, and the wielding rather than shrinking of government action, in the record of Ronal Reagan. Reagan stands as the chief deity in neoliberal ideology and is replayed as a central figure in Republican campaigns over the last several election cycles (at federal and state levels). Reagan perhaps more than anyone is invoked as the icon of "small government" and reduced state involvement in the economy. And Reagan's approach has provided the template for Crisis State governance by governments of all stripes (Clinton, Bush, Obama, Blair, Cameron, etc.) since. Indeed his name even formed the basis for an alternative designation of neoliberal economics — Reaganomics (which was initially more popular and widely used than the now more common term). Perhaps more memorably, this early presentation of neoliberalism was given the name "voodoo economics" by none other than Reagan's erstwhile opponent, later running mate and successor, George H.W. Bush.

Yet even a cursory glance at his actual record shows the deified icon of Reaganomics to be a complete distortion, a fabrication which rewrites the history of Crisis State governance under Reagan. Of all of the hallmarks of Reagan's vision, less government, less taxation, fiscal responsibility, privatization, and social service cuts, only the latter two were delivered. Perhaps it was voodoo economics after all.

The real story is telling if one looks at economic issues under Reagan. When Reagan entered office in January of 1981, the top tax rate was 70 percent. When he left it had been reduced to 28 percent (Spicer 2012). The result of tax breaks to the wealthy was a reduction in federal government revenue from those sources. But Reagan did not reduce the government budget. He actually sought to increase federal revenues but did so on the backs of the working class rather than capital (and his business allies). He increased payroll taxes as well as the rate on the lowest two quintiles. Far from being a tax-cutting hero as the mythology insists, Reagan actually raised taxes eleven times over the course of his terms in office (Seitz-Wald 2011). Reagan actually raised taxes in seven of the eight years he was in office, and these tax increases were felt most severely and painfully by the lower and middle income strata of the working class. Increased taxes on the working class coupled with cuts to essential services and programs needed by the working class served as dual pincers of austerity, crisis, anxiety, and desperation.

Reagan was also largely responsible for the US debt crisis, which resulted from his fiscal policies and particularly his ideological commitment to cut taxes for the wealthy. When Reagan came into office the national debt was $900 billion, that following a recession, but by the time he left the US national debt had tripled to $2.8 trillion (Noble n.d.). This, of course, provided a boon to bankers while serving as a powerful ideological justification to impose more austerity and crisis on the working class and poor. In terms of spending, in 1985 Federal outlays were 22.9 percent GDP, marking the highest over the period from 1962 to the George W. Bush era (Spicer 2012).

All of this was matched with increases in unemployment under Reagan. The unemployment rate jumped from 7.5 percent when he took office to 11 percent a year later, before Reagan infamously changed the way in which unemployment was measured in order to make the rates look less dire. When employment did pick up it was largely represented through a conversion of better-paying secure jobs into lower-paying, insecure service sector jobs.

Reagan's activism also included, perhaps most impactfully, his attack on unions. Mere months after taking office, in August 1981, Reagan intervened in the air traffic controllers' dispute, acting overtly on behalf of capital. Despite neoliberal claims that government must stay out of the economy and let the "invisible hand" decide, Reagan openly sided with business and fired 11,345 PATCO (Professional Air Traffic Controllers Organization) workers for not ending their strike and returning to work.

Yet, despite distortions in the historical remembrance, these are all bedrock components of Crisis State management. And they represent fundamentally a social re-engineering and a redistribution of social wealth upwards. And the state, far from being reduced or withdrawn, has been the key tool for effecting all of this social re-jigging.

Under the Crisis State "the governmental apparatus is dissolved in so far as it serves popular purposes, but maintained or enlarged as the coercive and administrative arm of capital" (Dyer-Witheford 1999, 102). Thus under austerity regimes military and police budgets grow. Reagan the neoliberal cost cutter, showing the Crisis State commitment to the martial apparatus of the state, also massively expanded defense spending by over $100 billion a year to a level not seen in the US since the height of the Vietnam war. It was Reagan the government reducer who added the Department of Veterans Affairs with a budget close to $90 billion.

The neoliberal government shrinkers, from Reagan on, oversee a massive growth in the penal apparatus, such that one now speaks of a prison industrial complex (PIC) and a carceral society. This reflects the cynical dual logic of Crisis State arrangements in which people are rendered more and more precarious, and thus more needing of surveillance, regulation, and containment within a broadened and interlinked carceral apparatus. In Dyer-Witheford's terms:

As whole strata of the population are cut off from support, potential social disorder is kept in check by the technologically intensive policing applied against the poor, indigent, and ghettoized. Around those convicted of transgression, the web of informational control tightens inexorably. (1999, 102)

This brings together simultaneous processes of poor bashing and racialized repression. False crises are manufactured around issues like welfare fraud, social assistance "scroungers," aggressive panhandling, etc. These fake crises are used as reasons to cut social spending on welfare policies (welfare, subsidized housing, rent controls, etc.) that benefit the working class but also as excuses to extend surveillance and regulation of those same individuals and communities. Thus in several jurisdictions social welfare cuts are shadowed by large increases in spending on surveillance, monitoring, and regulatory mechanisms to oversee and investigate the poor and welfare recipients. These include obnoxious developments like welfare snitch lines set up so that neighbors and family members can rat out people for cheating the system. Notably these snitch lines have found virtually no evidence for welfare fraud (costing several times more to set up than is ever recovered).

At the same time these practices are often deployed through racialized, and outright racist, discourses. Thus neoliberal cuts to welfare in the 1980s and 1990s were accompanied by racist myths such as the "welfare queen" for which Reagan provided the template in his election campaign against Carter. This was adopted and the ante upped under Bush I as the additional peril of "crack babies" was added on. These mythologies, in addition to ideologically buttressing calls to cut social services for the working classes, also provide supporting imagery for the war on drugs launched against poor and racialized communities and the ongoing crisis this has imposed on those communities and their members.

Negri (1988) also applies Marcuse's reference to the transition from "welfare state to warfare state" in describing the transition from the Planner State to the Crisis State. Can one really be too surprised that if one wages a "war on drugs" or a "war on poverty" that one will end up with militarized policing and armored vehicles moving against local domestic populations?

These interlocking processes of manufacturing crisis are extended in the expansion of the carceral framework and mass incarceration. This includes three strikes legislation and mandatory sentences. It also, in a way that again shows the economic impetus for accumulation and exploitation that are always part of Crisis State arrangements, effects the privatization of the penal system as reflected in the growth of private prisons and prison industries (where exploitation is restored to absolute slave-like levels). Recent analysts of carceral society, such as Dominque Moran and Hadar Aviram, remark on the curious fact that in a society obsessed with cost-benefit calculations that frame ideational values, social responsibility, and public priorities almost entirely as matters of concern over public spending there has been so little attention over decades of collective investment (in the billions) in the prison industrial complex, and much of that attention only more recently.

The fundamental outcome has been the Crisis State centerpiece of increased economic inequality and the massive, and growing, gap between rich and poor. As David Leonhardt of the New York Times has noted, "Since 1980, median household income has risen only 30 percent, adjusted for inflation, while average incomes at the top have tripled or quadrupled" (2010). The systematic growth in social inequality and division of society into a one percent of wealth and a 99 percent of precarity, to use the language of the Occupy Movement, is the very heart of Crisis State manipulation.

The lean, or better, crisis state is incapable of offering much in the way of actual security or certainty so it compensates with a zealous focus on safety, but only specific types of safety for specific citizens. Most common is the safety for consumers to consume (or perverse distortions of the security of workers to work for minimal wages under horrible conditions as in so-called "right to work" states).

The crisis of neoliberalism suggests the margin of a new cycle of the central control of economies (Negri 2008, 198). It may be more public and more common. Neoliberalism shows exactly the contrary of what it hopes to demonstrate. The problems of management of the economy, as well as society, become fundamental under neoliberalism. Neoliberalism's crisis owes not only to economic disequilibrium (that its policies and programs create) but also to its unilateral American political management globally. For Negri, "It's a crisis that determines conditions that capitalism can't manage any longer. We are at the point of a cyclic specific phase that started with Thatcher and [Ronald] Reagan, against which everything now declares war" (2008, 197). Neoliberal control of economic development, despite its rather self-serving boasts, is extremely limited.

Governance and Resistance:
From Planning (to) Crisis

Liberal forms of governing are not purely top-down and repressive. They involve people governing themselves and those around them. In this sense governance is self-replicating, self-(re)producing (Lorey 2015, 35). Self-government occurs through participation, not solely in politics, but in living. People are involved in self-government in the way they live. They *embody* liberal democratic forms of governing (Lorey 2015, 35). As Lorey suggests, "It is precisely through the way they conduct themselves, how they govern themselves, that individuals become amenable to social, political and economic steering and regulation" (2015, 35). Yet, these ways of living are, to be sure, structured and framed by instituted authorities and powerholders and, under capitalist relations, relate especially to capitalist forms of valorization.

Planner State arrangements included practices of self-governing which were, to be sure, geared toward the capitalist "free market" and economic rationalization. Thus, self-governance comes to be oriented around consumerist practices (various "self help" schemes but also a commodified version of the "good life" itself). And this is accompanied by, indeed underwritten by, a fidelity to the labor market and waged labor and the acceptance of state capitalist claims on social ownership.

This is reflected too in the historic postwar compromise with capital by mainstream union movements. In exchange for increased wages, benefits, vacations, etc. — the good life operationalized — unions dropped claims on capital, ownership, or workers' control of industry (and the end of exploitation). In virtually all union contracts of the period unions even gave up the fundamental right to withdraw labor according to the direct needs of workers themselves. This was expressed in provisions prohibiting wildcat strikes during the life of the contract.

Practices of self-discipline and self-governance play important parts in the Planner State arrangements, as part of the compromise against sectoral precarity undertaken by waged labor and the unions. Thus, it did not first take hold as a regulating principle under neoliberalism (Lorey 2015, 28).

Indeed it could be said that the self-discipline and self-governance that took hold in working class consciousness (and conscience) under Planner State arrangements helps us to understand the restricted and constrained opposition to neoliberal austerity over the first few decades of its imposition. Many activists from the 1980s on have expressed their exasperation with the timidity of opposition and its adherence to legal forms (elections, protests, demonstrations, petitions, lobbying) even as defeat piled on (self)defeat. The internalization of self-discipline (along lines of what stand as bourgeois morality) also helps shed light on the too-ready acceptance of conciliatory overtures and slight reforms (even as they are routinely not delivered or are simply rolled back).

This again raises the question of the power, the necessity, of rule breaking, of lawbreaking, and illegalism in resistance and struggle against domination in the current period of crisis and precarity. Under Crisis State conditions there grows an excess of what cannot be controlled. There is an excess of what goes beyond regulation. The uncontrollable or ungoverned challenge the social order. As obedience is delinked from protection and security the ranks of the uncontrollable pose new challenges for the state.

Crisis States and Precarity for All

Under the Planner State arrangements the threatening Other was relegated to the margins — rendered precarious as means of securing the welfare state. As Lorey puts it:

> Within the framework of its welfare-state paradigm of protection, liberal governmentality was based on multiple forms of precarity as inequality through *othering*: on the one hand, on the unpaid labour of women in the reproduction area of the private sphere; on the other hand, on the precarity of all those excluded from the nation-state compromise between capital and labour — whether an as abnormal foreign or poor — as well as those living under extreme conditions of exploitation in the colonies. (2015, 36)

Under the Planner State these were the precarized. These were also, to use the language of criminology, the general deterrence example. That is, the specified precarized stood as the example with which the partially secured could be threatened. There but for the grace of the state go you.

The institutions of the Planner State were not geared toward the security of workers as is often imagined (particularly by nostalgic social democrats today) but instead to support "economically productive self-government techniques among obedient and cautious citizens, who ensured themselves and precarized others simultaneously" (Lorey 2015, 39). Many were excluded from or left out of security, or provided inadequate care, in the welfare state (including the poor, homeless, women, migrants, indigenous people most of all).

Under Crisis States the precarized have been moved to the center. Or, more fully, precarity has become the norm (Lorey 2015, 39). Crisis States render precarity and the conditions of individual and collective insecurity as means of universal regulation and governance.

It was only in the last half of the twentieth century in certain jurisdictions that waged labor became associated with some sense of security within the framework of the welfare states in those countries. This security took a legislative form of access to limited rights of citizenship, sometimes referred to as social citizenship.

Crisis States restore waged labor to the realm of insecurity and despair. The breakup of welfare state provisions renders labor as subject entirely to the laws of the capitalist market — its abject condition historically.

The Crisis State is geared toward a regulation of social life based on dependence and desperation. This structures a source of labor with options, dependent on *any* "success" on the labor market for uncertain survival (without the slight fallback of the welfare state provisions). This in turn establishes and undergirds processes of exploitation and capital accumulation at renewed levels and intensities.

One is faced not with the promise of inclusive social welfare but rather of a state of bare life. The prospects of homelessness and poverty, and increasingly criminalization and detention, are explicitly placed before the working class without reservation or remorse.

Managed precarity is linked with extensions of repressive forms of power and control. This is seen in the mechanisms of the carceral state and campaigns such as the "war on drugs" or "broken windows" policing. It is also expressed in the proliferation of absurd legislation such as that which criminalizes survival strategies of the poor and/or homeless, such as anti-panhandling or anti-window squeegeeing laws. Among the most mean-spirited are laws against binning or dumpster diving, suggesting that even capital's property claims over garbage are worth more than the lives of the poor.

Those left precarious under the Planner State are not properly understood as excluded. Rather, the issue is still the nature of their inclusion. And they are centrally included, particularly within systems of criminalization, punishment, and repression. Indeed, as I have suggested elsewhere, contemporary systems of criminal justice in Western liberal democracies like Canada and the US would collapse without the processing of poor people (almost always for non-violent crimes, usually for victimless crimes, increasingly for bureaucratic or administrative "crimes" like failing to appear for court dates).

Conclusion

Crisis States throw liberal governance on its head. Rather than governing through the promise (not necessarily met) of protection, it governs through the production of social insecurity. It offers the associated justification, famous since Thatcher, of "no alternative."

As Judith Butler notes, precarity is not simply a passing or momentary condition. Rather, it is a new form of regulation that marks the current period of development (2015, vii). Precarity has become a regime of governance. It is by now a hegemonic mode of regulation and control (2015, vii).

Precarity and insecurity have from the start been central conditions of life for the working class and subordinate groups under capitalism. Indeed precarity and insecurity were necessary conditions for the emergence and expansion of capitalism. This is what enclosure of the commons and associated successive laws such as Poor Acts were deployed to effect, to enforce dependence on labor markets for survival, for example.

Neoliberal austerity was initially deployed to break the social resources, infrastructures, and bases for resistance built up by the working class over the period of struggles in the post-war period (which found state response in the mechanisms of the Planner State). This includes, front and center, the well coordinated and aggressive attacks on unions especially but also urban policing precarizing the poor and border controls and criminalization of migrant labor.

Its neoliberal character is precisely an attempt to restore conditions of capitalist dominance and working class insecurity as obtained in the early periods of so-called *laissez faire* capitalism. So we want to be cautious in not overstating the novelty of austerity and precarity when considering essential conditions of capital accumulation and exploitation.

At the same time, we recognize that *laissez faire* has always been an inaccuracy. The capitalist market has required state involvement and action, state management. There has never been a capitalist market free of the state despite the ideological effluence of Republican or Conservative Party "libertarians."

As Lorey suggests, precarization in the present period is not an exception, something outsourced to the periphery. It has become the rule. We might add — it has become the rule *again*. Precarity extends beyond the loss of waged employment; it speaks to more than insecure or temporary jobs. Rather, it now "embraces the whole of existence, the body, modes of subjectivation" (Lorey 2015, 1).

Under the Crisis State, precarity, as Lorey suggests, becomes normalized. Or to put it another way: "In neoliberalism precarization becomes 'democratized'" (Lorey 2015, 11). Under the Crisis State fears of job loss, fears of unemployment are everyday. Fears of not being able to pay the rent, feed the kids, pay for health, dental, eye care, press even for those who are employed. As Paolo Virno notes, anxieties are felt within community that were typically felt outside of community (2004, 33).

Indeed, Agamben (1996) proposes the refugee, the non-status, as the paradigmatic political subjectivity of contemporary life and politics. The segmentation of the workforce between national and foreign workers, citizens and non-status, has seriously weakened the political power of workers. The condition of being non-status has been experienced both in terms of the labor market and in terms of the response from unions.

This raises important questions for resistance and the opposition to crisis. On one hand it poses a commons of experience in precarity that poses opportunities for shared struggle. At the same time it can impel a rupture with the conditions of crisis in splitting communities from the prospect of positive resolution, of satisfaction, within the context of the current arrangements. All of this is laid bare in recent struggles, from Idle No More to #BlackLivesMatter to the new poor people's movements of various types in countries across the neoliberal democratic West, which make explicit the incapacity of the system to meet their demands, and indeed raise the undesirability of attempts at accommodation and recuperation which do not fundamentally disrupt and alter existing institutions and power and authority.

ON RESISTANCE IN A TIME OF CRISIS: WE ARE ALL ILLEGAL NOW

THE NORMALIZATION OF CRISIS ALSO serves to open specific opportunities for people to refuse existing forms of governance (Lorey 2015, 4). Possibilities for organization and resistance under Crisis State capitalism are on a different footing than occurs during the arrangements of the welfare state period. In the Crisis State period, "a new population presents itself that wants to reaffirm the capacity of expressing itself democratically against the war that is coming, against the new totalitarian media organization of the social, against the precaritization that is promoted" (Negri 2008, 94). This includes moves beyond political representation through direct action and direct democracy, rather than the mediation of electoralism and parliamentarism. It also involves the direct presentation of needs and desires, including through self-produced means of expression (activist media, indymedia, etc.).

Some of the most provocative challenges to capital and states have come from collective resistance among the diverse precarious. These include uprisings of the poor, movements against detention and deportation, indigenous movements. And notably the new uprisings and mobilizations against crsis have been driven by their needs rather than the limits of legality and so-called civil protest. They overflow the bounds of dissent as an act of citizenship or action permissible to instituted authorities. The new movements pursue an illegalism that takes its lead from the needs of participants rather than the preferences or priorities of the state. They do not let the authorities define or limit their actions in the manner of symbolic protest or civil disobedience.

Unlike the managerial search for inclusion and legalistic obedience of relations under the Planner State, it must express disobedience of the precarious. These refusals, this uncivil disobedience, becomes important in rethinking resistance.

No Way Back Machine:
The Planner State and Its Nostalgists

The Planner State management of insecurity provided a bulwark against the prospect of revolt or insurrection. One effect, significantly, of the Planner State is to undermine the autonomy of the working class and to bring its class institutions within a legalistic framework. This is perhaps most notable in the legal framework for union recognition. In Planner State arrangements, the trade union is recognized and gains standing purely within a legislative framework of legal bargaining over specific forms of a labor contract and so-called collective bargaining. Part of this is to ensure the limitation of labor's demands to those of technocrats (rather than social considerations of working-class communities) — such as hourly wage, job description, some conditions of layoff, etc. The contract form also, fundamentally, asserts the right of capital to ownership and control of the workplace and its products. Crucially, the working class abandons its claims of ownership and control — and over time even forgets that such claims are part of its history, its entitlement.

Even more, the working class gives up its foundational power to stop work — it gives up the right to wildcat (unannounced, unregulated) strikes. Strikes, the right and capacity to withdraw labor, are reduced to pre-announced, pre-arranged, pre-scheduled, permitted events, limited in duration, location, and intensity. Precisely so bosses can prepare for a strike (by stocking supplies or building up product), ahead of time. Strikes become legal in form — stipulating when and where they can occur and who might participate. This is a reworking of the very idea of collective action and labor power. For this reworking (a capitulation) labor receives in return no equivalent.

More than this though, the Planner State arrangements build working-class dependence on the capitalist state for the provision of necessary, essential, resources — in healthcare, education, elder care, child care, housing, etc. This process of dependence has been examined in detail by the anarchist Colin Ward. As Alan Sears suggests, one of the main factors in the decline of working-class infrastructures of resistance has been the so-called success of the working class (in limited and legalistic terms).

Despite the longing and wistful nostalgia of too much of the Left (despite repeated failures and disappointments, from the New Democratic Party (NDP) in Canada to the Workers' Party (PT) in Brazil to Syriza in Greece), there is no return to the Planner State to be had. No way back to the future. As Lorey suggests, "There is no longer a centre or a middle that could be imagined as a society stable enough to take in those pushed to the margins. In the context of the current economic and political crises it is no longer sufficient to demand an equal, pluralistic society on republican foundations" (2015, 60–61). This is true both because it is clear in the context of Crisis States that capital will not allow it and because it cannot even begin to meet the social or environmental needs of the subjugated. The terms of settlement are off and there is no appetite (or reason) for capital to pursue or accept something along the lines of the welfare state compromise. Neither is there a reason for contemporary movements to set their sights so low, to follow a false path.

The idea that there can be a just and egalitarian management of capitalism remains, as Negri puts it, a mad idea. Capital cannot survive without exploitation. Socialists mistakenly thought there could be a just measure of exploitation. And their remnants in social democratic parties, social reform movements, and NGOs still do. This has been their futile pursuit over three decades of neoliberalism.

The Western socialists and social democrats have remained Stalinists but are not socialists anymore. They went from the fetishization of the Soviet Union to complete abandonment of any possibility of the transformation of life and society. They gave a bureaucratic interpretation to the ideas and expressions of "real socialism." This has now turned to cynicism (Negri 2008).

From 1968, famously, people in the West "start to consider the possibility of producing wealth and freedom at the same time" (Negri 2008, 23). The socialists arrive at the same point in 1989, but, overcome by events, they become unambiguous apologists for capitalism (Negri 2008, 25).

The social democratic Frankenstein attempts to revive a dead corpse shows the Left adheres to the internal logic of crisis and domination. States of all stripes fear any sense of rupture. They prefer transition. The focus of states is governance rather than politics.

"We Are Ungovernable": Terms of Refusal

The decades of austerity governance under the Crisis State shows clearly the end of a social democratic rapprochement with capital. The terms have changed, largely in benefit of capital, and the social result for the subjugated has been a regression to the terms of early *laissez faire* conditions. At the same time, however, "this regression, bringing with it huge increases in poverty rates, social polarization, and general human suffering, has catalyzed opposition" (Dyer-Witheford 1999, 102). This is the field of precarious capitalism and of movements against precarity.

Among the most notable forms of resistance have been the variety of "new poor people's movements that have emerged since from the late 1980s to today in response, partly, to the intensifying destruction of social safety nets" (Dyer-Witheford

1999, 103). In the context of Western liberal democracies some of the most inspiring and informative examples include the anti-borders movements of immigrants and refugees, movements against eviction and foreclosure, direct action anti-poverty movements, and the movements against police violence in poor racialized neighborhoods. These forces have found expression in virtually every country of North American and Europe, from the Ontario Coalition Against Poverty in Canada to the *indignados* in Spain. Uprisings against colonial impoverishment of indigenous communities have erupted in and against all settler colonial states.

Significantly, these movements have refused confinement within the parameters of actions/activism considered appropriate for "responsible citizens." Beyond the civil disobedience characteristic of many new social movements, these new poor people's movements have developed and practiced a diverse repertoire of "uncivil practices." This expresses a growing awareness of the limitations of state-centered and legalistic actions within the context of precarious capitalism and Crisis States. As Del Re suggests, "Protesting by using the language of rights obviously means asking the State's permission for protection. 'Rights' are invoked, contested, distributed, and protected, but also limited and appointed by the law" (1996, 107). Within the new poor people's movements, the symbolic action and march have been replaced by "multiple, small-scale, 'in-yer-face' actions" (McKay 1998, 269, n.4). As McKay has noted with reference to the rise of direct action politics in the earlier period of neoliberalism:

> Activism means action: whereas in earlier decades opposition to, say, a construction project or an industrial pollutant might have meant a group standing at the gates handing out leaflets, today it is more likely to be voiced by invading the offices and disrupting work, trashing the computers and throwing files out the windows. (1998, 5)

Notably, actions that move beyond the bounds of state and capitalist permissibility raise important prospects for understanding and acting against interlocked systems of exploitation and oppression. Particular struggles may link up "as part of a practical critique of the whole capital relation" (*Aufheben* 1998, 105). They raise the contradiction between the values of communities (in care) of the subjugated and the state capitalist drive for value (in exploitation).

> Such struggles may be both valid in their own right (that is they satisfy our immediate needs as opposed to those of capital) *and* point directly to a higher level of struggle; a victory *may create new needs and desires* (which people then feel confident to set about satisfying) and *new possibilities* (which make the satisfaction of these and other needs and desires more likely), and so on. (*Aufheben* 1998, 105)

Direct action and disruptive politics base opposition on the self-directed power of the subjugated themselves rather than on an imagined representation from elsewhere (in the form of instituted authorities or experts). "What both leftist and eco-reformist positions have in common is that they both look outside ourselves and our struggles for the real agent of change, the real historical subject: leftists look to 'the party' while eco-reformists look to parliament" (*Aufheben* 1998, 106). The direct actionists assert a do-it-ourselves ethos. The political significance of disruptive politics is found less in the immediate aims of particular actions or in the immediate costs to capital and the state but "more in our *creation of a climate of autonomy, disobedience and resistance*" (*Aufheben* 1998, 107). This is building, through experience, a capacity for struggle and capacity for realizing alternatives.

As British autonomist paper *Aufheben* (1998, 107–108) has noted with respect to squatting, "Moreover, a situation without the dull compulsion of rent, work, bills, and so on, provided the basis for creating and reinventing a community, which, in turn, encouraged other ideas." In sum, this daily existence of thoroughgoing struggle was simultaneously a *negative* act (stopping the road, etc.) and a *positive pointer* to the kind of social relations that could exist: no money, the end of exchange values, communal living, no wage labor, no ownership of space (*Aufheben* 1998, 110). No representative or legalistic forms of politics can approach this capacity building and experience in making practical alternatives real in the materiality of everyday life.

The new movements become uncontrollable for the instituted mechanisms of governance. They are unpredictable and autonomous. This makes them frightening for the state. The uncontrollable raise the specter of rupture, of *scission*. They pose the prospect, most frightening for the state, of secession. These groups hold a potential to take down the whole social structure (Castel 1995).

Popular actions and uprisings are, by definition, illegal. In the occupations in disparate global sites people collectively resolved "insoluble problems without the help of the state" (Badiou 2012, 111). Freely associating, they constitute themselves, their creative power, without the state. Affinity replaces coercion.

A Note on Violence

Riots are promising in that they hold things as they are, current conditions, as intolerable, unreformable, irremedial, unacceptable, and (most dangerous of all for authorities of all stripes) as beyond compromise. In reality, it is more important, for the moment, to make it impossible for the police to act, to show the capacity to resist the state of siege. Resistance to the state of siege raises important problems of strategy to be addressed. Emerging infrastructures of resistance must be prepared and capable of defending themselves, both against physical assault and against cooptation or incorporation. The state responses are about governance rather than public security.

Perhaps the most striking example of riotous opposition and insurrectionary impulse, at least in Western liberal democracies, is provided by the black bloc tactic during street demonstrations. The black bloc offers a step beyond both the reformism or protest politics and the authoritarian permissibility of legalistic *civil* disobedience. The black bloc, in which all participants dress in black and cover their faces to avoid surveillance and criminalization while engaging in whatever actions are deemed necessary to bring ruling authorities to crisis, visually show unity in diversity and solidarity in action. They act according to their needs and desires rather than the limits of what police deem to be acceptable "protest" routine or ritual.

For Negri, the black bloc are mistaken. In his view they represent a Nietzschean solitary revolt, which, while morally efficacious, always loses politically (Negri 2008, 96). His concern is not with their revolt, but results from the fact that they do not revolt with others in the movement. Rather, "they revolt against the others with a claim of purity, and individualist height that isolates them. In this individual isolation of rebellion I don't see reconstruction" (Negri 2008, 97). In as sense, while their actions might be correct, they stand alone. They do not allow a positive recomposition of oppositional fighting force. In Negri's view:

> I am against the individualism of rebellious action just as much as possessive individualism. I maintain that the renewal of the movements is always collective in any form and in any movement of their recomposition. The figure of the industrial worker, of the proletariat, of the exploited worker doesn't exist if not in a collective form. Nobody was ever exploited alone. (2008, 96)

So too are the actual impacts of the black bloc limited. They also represent an individual, an isolated, scream of anger and outrage. They do not pose the broad and antisystemic force of proletarian uprising, even of a workplace strike. The damage of the black bloc needs to be put in proper context, not only with the violence of the state and corporations, but in relation to recent forms of proletarian violence. The events in Paris, the uprisings in the *banlieues,* showed the real extent of the black bloc actions: "thirty cars in three days in Genoa, while in Paris more than fifteen hundred in a single night of urban jacquerie" (Negri

2008, 97). The point here is an important one and speaks to the character of urban uprisings based in the actions of the subjugated in their neighborhoods and on behalf of their own needs rather than the angry dissatisfaction of the protester or activist.

Yet debates over the black bloc within movements are significant and stand for something more. The polemics over the black bloc are, more importantly, expressing a theme of the expulsion of violence from the movements. In Genoa violence was applied by the movement beyond the black blocs, yet some argued still for non-violence or "passive violence," much as they had in Quebec City. There is a strong idea that movements should not express a violence that goes beyond passive resistance. For Negri, this is "false theoretically and historically, morally and politically" (2008, 98). The notion of resistance without violence is a distortion of history and an effect of power that reinforced power.

Such illegalist moments and movements are subjected to various practices of repression and recuperation. Various attempts are made "to bring back into an institutional framework the scandalous phenomena of 'no-go areas,' behaviors or territories that defy the logic of the police and the marketplace, and ask to be recognized and legitimated above all at the material and symbolic level" (Illuminati 1996, 177). This includes moral regulation and the spectacle of moral panics against insubordinates of various types. It, of course includes, the moralizing punishment of police actions in the streets (violence against rebels as a means of taming them and those who are watching and otherwise inspired by them) and the patronizing lectures of police press conferences afterwards.

It also includes, perhaps less recognized and remarked upon, the sanctimonious and self-satisfied actions of other movement participants. This takes the form of an "internal policing" of the movements and is at least as fatal for resistance as the external policing of the cops. Thus one hears after almost every direct action or disruptive demonstration the condemnations of the "peaceful protesters" and fundamentalists of civil disobedience. Playing the role of public relations specialists for the state and capital, these "reasonable activists" work to delegitimize direct actionists and insurrectionists in the eyes of the public while simultaneously presenting law and order and legalistic frameworks as the only proper and acceptable terms of dissent, thus posing legitimate opposition as always only a loyal opposition.

As Negri has stated forcefully, and rightly, "A Left that imagines movements without the capacity to express themselves in a violent way falsifies reality and mystifies the nature of the movements" (2008, 98). Violence simply happens. It is a part of the material existence of human relations. According to Negri, "My apology for violence is anything other than an apology of criminal acts, or of those predisposed to hurt the other. I only say that to eliminate violence from the political debate is banal, like thinking of being able not to eat and drink. Violence is part of human reality" (2008, 99). Social relations are violent, but not necessarily because people want it. It is not to say that violence has to be presented as a necessary element in the construction of an alternative society. At the same time, for Negri, in exodus there is always need of a rear guard that can combat where needed.

Negri makes the crucial point, often obscure to modern-day would-be revolutionaries who see themselves as players in a historical drama, that the *coup d'état,* the overthrow of the state by a violent minority, is not part of the communist project in the current context. What does it mean to eliminate violence from social relations in the current context of the state of permanent exception? Those who want to expel violence from class relations are either reactionaries or revisionists. For Negri, the Left has never managed to achieve a "realistic analysis of violence" (2008, 100). Yet communism as the transformation of reality is not constituted primarily through instrumental violence. According to Negri, "Only in the most acute revolutionary periods has it been shown to be joyous, because its power consisted in making death distant" (2008, 100). That is, violence of the subjugated is deployed against a normalized violence that is not even taken as such. This can include the unnamed class violence of hunger and homelessness or the more obvious class violence of police killings and militarization.

The times for action have changed. As Negri puts it, "The conquest of the Winter Palace today doesn't have anything to do anymore with the communist project. The problem seems to me to be another one. It consists in the common and in the exercise of the common" (2008, 99). This is a positive and constructive practice, building infrastructures, ensuring survival, rather than a destructive one. The new violence is generalized and present everywhere. In response, resistance appears as exodus, the "leaving of this world" (Negri 2008, 101). Yet the new world cannot be constructed by pretending that there is not violence (Negri 2008, 101).

With the socialist dictators violence entered "the sadness of power" once more as the difference disappeared between the way in which the socialist parties understood violence and the way it was interpreted by the capitalists and their governments (Negri 2008, 100). The thing that is crucial to emphasize in any historical analysis is not the madness of domination but the force of resistance (Negri 2008).

Coming Together:
New Recompositions

The alter movements are for a collective action. The destructive refrain requires a revolutionary process. Precarity, austerity, and crisis provide bases for new alliances. These alliances are asserting relations of communal care and refusing the dividing logics of protection and security for some, on a hierarchical basis, but not for others (Lorey 2015, 91). The affective labor, highlighted in neoliberal capitalist production processes, redeployed now, becomes a starting point for connections with others that break the isolation of crisis conditions.

The precarious cannot be unified and represented in traditional political forms. By definition the precarious are diverse and dispersed. They are so in the many fields of production in which they labor. They come from disparate, migrant backgrounds and work in diverse fields. They labor in temporary jobs. They are also dispersed in life. Often they must travel long distances for jobs (within a locale or to other locales). There is often great separation between home and work life. Often they are excluded from, or unknown to, social service agencies (those of social welfare rather than of criminalization).

And traditional organizations of representation, from unions to political parties, have abandoned or overlooked much of the precarious (migrants, homeless, service sector workers, those in small workplaces, etc.). New politics and political forms already show that they eschew the traditional forms of representational politics. As Lorey points out, "What is obvious is that the contemporary normalization of precarization substantially challenges established forms of politics. It is not only the capitalist mode of production that finds itself in special crisis; the fundamental crisis of modes of political representation also becomes conspicuous" (2015, 61). Precarity is now taken as a reality for political mobilization and connection. There is no assumption that deliverance from precariousness is in the offing, to be delivered through the institutions of the social welfare state.

The new movements are shifting the grounds of political action. The recomposition of forces occurs on a basis of participatory horizontalism and decentralization. It moves beyond the terms of welfare state inclusion/exclusion and suggests new solidarities. As Negri argues, "Another fact is the radical egalitarianism that increasingly emerges, beginning from the base with the demand for the rights of immigrants or the social wage for precarious workers. In short, the opening of the borders and implicit cosmopolitanism" (2008, 27). The demands are at the base of a sort of new enlightenment for commentators like Negri. This is a biopolitical enlightenment that exposes new concepts of reason. This is not a functional or instrumental "superannuation of the capitalist order" but a concrete transition "of solidarity in the biological perspective" (Negri 2008, 28). Negri argues:

However, the new labor power and the men who live reading in the common their desire for happiness (I mean the
proletariat of immaterial and precarious labor, cognitive
and affective today) feel violence like the arms of those who
command them, as continual expropriation — increasingly
unjustified — of their knowledge, as power that cuts the soul
and every vital substance. (2008, 101)

The current period is a transition of classes and the general
forms of governance of empire. For the global multitudes it is
uncertain what the articulations between the "migratory movements and multitudinous structures" will be (Negri 2008, 101).
What is the common ground between the socially precarious
and the migrants? What does it mean "to bring together precarious intellectuals, old mass workers, and immigration" (Negri 2008, 101)? For Negri: "At the limit, they can represent two
opposed points: the migrant is the hero of spatial mobility, while
the precarious worker is the hero of temporal flexibility. But
what brought them together is capital" (2008, 101). This unification is a negative point that does not offer a clear political articulation of the two situations (Negri 2008, 102).

Alternative globalization demonstrations express a recomposition of the multitude (as diversity and singularity). For Negri,
"either singularity is shared or it becomes individualism, which
is something negative" (2008, 97). The specifity of each subjugation resonates through the generalization of precariousness.
The new egalitarianism is not about the flattening out of difference, it is not about the indistinct. As Negri suggests, "On the
contrary, it is open to singularities that live and produce within
this common network. To be equal is to have equal possibilities and capacities of expression that are effective and that exist
within the totality of the activities of the multitude" (2008, 28).
For Negri, "Production and freedom are born in the network.
The network is always a network of singularity, expression, and
production of differences" (2008, 28). It is, too, a production of
linkages of resonance.

Quebec City and Genoa were watershed moments (even if soon eclipsed by 9/11). They both represented a recomposition, a renovation for the movement of movements in the global North. With reference to Genoa, Negri suggests it announced neither a movement of class nor a student movement, a "new harlequin subject" (2008, 93). Such was also true of Quebec City. These were spaces on the making. For some they signaled the possibility of a new proletarian Left, which is "multitudinous, intellectual, precarious" (Negri 2008, 93). Genoa in the 1960s was the site of recognition of the mass worker (of *operaismo*), the port workers and the immigrant workers of the steel and auto industries. In Carlini Stadium, where the militants who came to Genoa met, there developed experiments of sharing rather than of leadership or technique. There were practices of a "regime of assemblage" (Negri 2008, 94). From this came the mass resistance to repression that followed as defense of the G8 became a "war of low intensity" or a form of "preventative war" (Negri 2008, 94).

It is a new proletarian Left that hints at recomposing in the renewed movements of precarity. The new mobilizations pose the possibility of resistance beyond the momentary uprisings that give public expression to them.

The biopower of the Crisis States must be confronted by new democratic (participatory) forms. As Negri notes, though, participation must be comprehended within mass solutions. This involves, of course, many transitions and levels (Negri 2008, 155–156). For Negri, "It is therefore in the liberation from exploitation and in the construction of the common that the poles of the political constitution are defined" (2008, 156). This is the impetus of commonism and new forms of political convergence through defense of the commons.

Toward the Positive in Struggle

Alain Badiou suggests that this "time of riots" signals nothing short of a rebirth of history. In his view, the urgent character of this time is more readily perceived by the ruling classes at present. And this is reflected in their constant anxiety and the obsessive approach to building up their weapons, both judicial and military (Badiou 2012, 5). The activity of the ruling classes makes it even more pressing that the working classes develop their own new future.

The apparent early victories in Tunisia and Egypt quickly re/turned to crises of their own for the popular constituents of the uprising. In Libya the risings were quickly sidelined by an imperialist invasion and restoration of local clientelism. In Syria the risings have been on the one hand (ISIS and the government war crimes) calamitous and on the other (Rojava and the anarchist fight in Kobanê) rich with historical possibilities (suggesting a new context). And these are contexts in which the mobilizations have been more militant and broader than in the Western liberal democracies.

The risings do show most of all that a popular action is always possible, even under awful circumstances. If the current risings against crisis in the Western liberal democracies have faltered, it is in part because they have so far been expressed in negative terms (no austerity, so-and-so out, *anti*-this or that, etc.). There has yet to emerge a positive (or various positives) that express a viable alternative around which popular risings might coalesce and advance. The negative is never enough. It cannot replace the positive and its organization. It cannot fire the radical imagination.

Even the Occupy movement, which did provide, if in limited form, some crystallization of an idea, was much better at expressing clearly what it opposed than a compelling alternative — a convincing positive (sadly, too few found the option of sitting in tents with minimal provision — usually brought by unionized workers — to be a gripping vision of a positive alternative future).

Unfortunately, even otherwise clear-sighted commentators like Badiou become too enamored of the apparently novel forms of occupations. They see perhaps too much in the occupation and hope they present a unification of diverse subjects in a historic force (which, in minimal ways, perhaps it does express). But this intense local presence never poses a material threat to the ruling executive (though to specific figures within it they might be — and those can be made expendable without any real change to the system and its crisis).

To destroy a bank is an eruption of insurrectionary joy. To destroy systems of banking is another matter. For Negri: "But first we need to understand how a society without banks functions, we need to invent a new reality for ourselves" (2008, 97). And this is the positive character of struggle.

THE POSITIVE CONTENT OF STRUGGLE: AUTO-VALORIZATION

THE STRUGGLES AGAINST CRISIS SEEK positive alternatives to the current context of oppositional struggles. The challenge as always is to move from refusal to assertion. While the antis (anticapitalism, antiracism, anticolonialism, etc.) are essential in forming bases of resistance, there is a growing need to offer compelling positives toward which resistance strives. This is the desire which is pressing so forcefully on the contemporary movements. A key part of this involves struggles over values, specifically the move to replace capitalist production of values with the social production of those values that sustain us and our communities.

Autonomist Marxist Harry Cleaver has given much attention to an examination of recent works, both within and outside of Marxist and anarchist theories, on what he terms "the positive content of working class struggle" or, more descriptively, "on the various ways in which people have sought to move beyond mere resistance to capitalism toward the self-construction of alternative ways of being" (1992, 106). It should be clear by now that the question of moving beyond resistance and toward the self-construction of alternatives, and indeed the relationships between the two, is the primary preoccupation of contemporary commonists and the concern that motivates much of their activity.

The self-construction of alternative ways of being is, of course, the central focus of the present work.

Auto-Valorization

The cycle of struggles of the late 1960s and early 1970s gave rise to perhaps the most serious attempts to conceptualize autonomous creativity as both a source of working class power and a potential movement beyond capitalism. Work by Italian Marxists such as Raniero Panzieri and Mario Tronti attempted to understand processes by which capitalist power could transform all of society into a "social factory," while at the same time seeking to analyze the potential for resistance posed by emerging acts of refusal within the working class.

Out of these attempts to theorize the development of working-class autonomy against capitalism, the Italian New Left Marxist Antonio Negri suggested the notion of working class *autovalorizzazione,* or what has been translated as auto-valorization or, perhaps more commonly, self-valorization (Cleaver 1992, 128–129). Negri's conceptualization of auto-valorization was an attempt to develop the understanding of the power of refusal to subvert capitalist domination and, significantly, to show how the power of refusal must be complemented by a power of constitution. The refusal of capitalist domination, or subsumption, is very closely related with the affirmative activities of self-valorization. The refusal of work is a necessary contributor to self-valorization in that it allows for the liberation of spaces that might then be filled through alternative, autonomous projects (Cleaver, 1992). As Cleaver suggests:

> If capital is successful in converting all of life into work there is no space or time or energy for self-valorisation. The refusal of work with its associated seizure of space (e.g. land, buildings) or time (e.g. weekends, paid vacations, non-work time on the job) or energy (an entropy raising diversion from

work) creates the very possibility of self-valorisation. (1992, 130)

Thus, under Crisis State conditions of austerity and precarity, insecurity of the labor market shapes opportunities for survival but also for resistance. Struggles over precarity more broadly and securing conditions of life and care become crucial. These become struggles over the nature of social value (and accumulation) itself. The structure of the wage, the division of labor, and surplus value are all mechanisms through which exploitation is organized (Cleaver 1992). And Crisis States, through neoliberal austerity, the restructuring of labor markets, the capital mobility of trade deals, and other polices, have facilitated shifts in all of these, benefiting capital while weakening labor. Especially exploitation, the extraction of surplus value, and opposition to exploitation must be returned to as a central focus of struggles against crisis.

From Value to Values

For autonomist Marxists, all aspects of capitalist society, and indeed all theoretical concepts used to explain such societies, bear a dual perspective depending on whether they are approached from the position of surplus value or from the position of surplus value as profit. As Marx of course suggested, capitalists view surplus value primarily as profit, and even more as profit in relation to investment. That is to say that capitalists are interested in surplus value not only as an absolute amount, but more importantly in terms of the amount of investment required to bring it about. Capitalists are, in other words, concerned with the rate of profit. This is one reason that ventures that are hugely profitable, in absolute terms, such as auto manufacturing, are closed down or moved to "more profitable" areas with lower labor or environmental costs, a characteristic feature of globalization. When the rate of profit in one sector becomes too low relative to investments, or cannot compare satisfactorily with the rate in other sectors or areas, capitalists will generally shift investment, even though absolute profits may have been quite high.

From the perspective of the working class, the key concerns over surplus value are vastly different than they are for capital. As Cleaver remarks:

> First, the absolute amount of surplus labour time being extracted from them is of great importance because it measures one part of the life time they give up to capital. Second, for workers the relevant measure of the relative size of surplus-value is not the rate of profit but the rate of exploitation, s/v, where the time given up to capital is compared to the time expended in meeting their own needs. (1992, 109)

Unwaged work, such as housework, has been subordinated to the reproduction of capital. This means that such work is diminished in terms of social recognition, either by states or by capital. The most important social labor is neither recognized nor funded (even at proper labor market value, let alone social value). It also means that the labor of care of the working class, because it is not compensated in a market economy, is often relegated to time left after paid labor is done.

As Cleaver (1992, 109) notes, the concept of surplus value and the concept of surplus value as profit represent different and opposed preoccupations related to specific class interests. Moreover, in the day-to-day affairs of capitalist society, this working-class perspective on surplus-value, where not entirely obliterated, is certainly obscured by the capitalist preoccupation with profit.

Working-class struggles against surplus value have taken, generally speaking, two primary forms. First are struggles to shorten the working day. These struggles include, for example, the historic anarchist and syndicalist battles for the eight-hour day or the five-day week. Such struggles cut *absolute* surplus value. The second major struggles center around attempts to increase the value of labor power. These involve the more familiar and ongoing efforts of the, especially mainstream, labor movements to increase wages. Such struggles cut *relative* surplus value. All of these struggles are geared towards, in some way, lowering the rate of exploitation (Cleaver 1992, 109).

Capitalist efforts to expand surplus value are primarily about increasing the rate of profit, and indeed this is largely what recent "innovations" around flexibilization, batch production and, more broadly, globalization itself, have been about. Battles over the length of the working day exemplify both workers' efforts to reduce their exploitation and capital's attempts to expand or maintain their profits (Cleaver 1992, 110). It is a struggle between the efforts of capitalists to dominate and of working-class resistance to that domination.

Marx's analysis of technological change, and its long-term consequences noted the tendency of capital to replace workers, who are less controllable, with controllable machinery. Italian New Left Marxists during the 1960s, including Panzieri and Tronti, analysed technological changes and the "modernization" of industry in terms of the capitalist use of machinery as means to control and further dominate the working class. This has, of course, amplified with computerization and the social media economies (first noted in the 1980s as so-called Benettonization or just-in-time production facilitated by computerized networks).

Mainstream unions have tended to join capital in trumpeting the supposed benefits of such change, especially the possibility of rising wages associated with increases in productivity, or "efficiency" in contemporary language. The Italian autonomists, however, suggested, what many rank-and-filers knew through experience, that such changes were used to increase exploitation and, even more, to weaken the power of workers (Cleaver 1992, 112). And this gave rise to open opposition among rank-and-file assembly line workers in the last years of the postwar Planner State arrangements. The autonomists simply gave a theoretical expression to an anger felt by rank-and-file workers of the period. This anger regularly expressed itself in the wildcat strikes and sabotage that marked industrial workplaces during the period of the late-1960s through the early 1970s.

If refusal offered a negative moment in the opposition to capitalist domination, auto-valorization expressed a positive aspect of struggle towards an alternative. This is a valorization that, as expressed in the prefix *auto* or *self,* is autonomous from capitalist valorization and, indeed, attempts to articulate a movement beyond solely resisting capitalist valorization. As Cleaver (1992) suggests, it is a self-defining and self-determining process that seeks to constitute something other than capital. What that "other than" is remains open to a great variety of responses. Indeed, self-valorization can be said to articulate simultaneously, as one recent popular expression puts it, "one no, many yeses." In Cleaver's terms:

> Alongside the power of refusal or the power to destroy capital's determination, we find in the midst of working-class recomposition the power of creative affirmation, the power to constitute new practices. In some cases, these autonomous projects are built on old bases, inherited and protected cultural practices from the past that have successfully survived capital's attempts at disvalorisation and devalorisation. In other cases, these projects are newborn, created fully formed out of appropriated elements which have hitherto been integral parts of capitalist accumulation. In such cases self-valorisation is not only autonomous from and opposed to valorisation but it can also be the converse of disvalorisation. It can include processes akin to what the Situationists used to call *"détournement"* or the diversion of elements of domination into vehicles of liberation. (1992, 130)

This has rather profound implications for rethinking how one might conceptualize communism. It certainly speaks against hegemonic notions of communism. For Cleaver:

> An important part of Negri's elaboration of the concept of self-valorisation is his recognition that, unlike valorisation

and unlike most socialist visualisations of communism, it does not designate the self-construction of a unified social project but rather denotes a "plurality" of instances, a multiplicity of independent undertakings not only in the spaces opened within and against capitalism but also in their full realization. (1992, 130)

Such a conceptualization is actually very close to the vision of communism put forward historically by anarchists. For anarchists, communism is viewed as decentralized, multiple groupings arranged as federations or networks.

Communism, viewed through the lens of self-valorization, then, is "thus not only a self-constituting praxis, but it is also the realisation of 'multilaterality' of the proletarian subject, or, better, of a subject which in its self-realisation explodes into multiple autonomous subjects" (Cleaver, 1992: 130). Note that this is a non- or, indeed, an anti-hegemonic politics. It expresses an emphasis on autonomy and solidarity rather than centralization and command. In the term used by anarchist Richard Day (2005), it affirms a politics of affinity. This is open and inclusive, multiplicity rather than singularity, agility rather than rigidity. These are hallmarks of the emergent politics against crisis. In Cleaver's view:

Against traditional socialist demands to subordinate difference to unity in the struggle against capital and in the construction of a unified post-capitalist order, [they] embrace what Negri calls the "multilaterality" of self-determination, the multiplicity of autonomous projects whose elaboration can constitute a new world whose "pluralism" would be real rather than illusory as is the case today in the world of capital. (1992, 132)

It is also a politics that breaks the bounds of rigid conceptualizations of what is meant by working class or by class struggle. On one hand it expresses an intersectionality of class exploitation and oppression on bases of racialization, patriarchy, sexual exclusion, colonialism, and nationality, among others. It also shifts understandings of production beyond traditionally understood workplaces. This includes a contextualization of the blue-collar working class, but also shifts attention from the factory to the social factory in the re/production of capital. Thus such an approach restores housework and so-called reproductive activities as well as marginalized activities of the lumpenproletariat (sex work, underground and informal economies, survival street work, etc.). As Cleaver notes:

> The concept has also proved flexible enough to be useful for understanding and appreciating struggles which have often been considered outside of the working class. These include not only the struggles of so-called urban "marginals" which have often been relegated to the "lumpenproletariat," but also a wide variety of peasant struggles. (1992, 130–131)

This fact helps, in part, to explain the enthusiasm that some anarchists have shown for the notion of self-valorization. Contemporary anarchists have, as earlier discussions have shown, generally identified with or more closely associated with struggles of the urban "marginals" or with peasant movements. At least as far back as Bakunin, who saw the "lumpenproletariat" rather than the industrial working class of Marxism as the most likely rebellious or revolutionary anti-capitalist class, anarchists have given serious attention and support to organizing among capitalism's poorest. Marx was himself famously dismissive of the lumpenproletariat, a group he viewed contemptuously as opportunistic mercenaries likely to betray the working class to the highest bidder. Such a view was taken up by generations of Marxists who viewed the poorest classes as, at best, powerless or ineffectual and, at worst, reactionary. As mentioned above ,anarchists have long been more interested in the revolutionary potential of peasant struggles than traditional Marxists who have dismissed such struggles as petit bourgeois or "backwards." The emergent movements against crisis impel a rethinking of such understandings of class (while retaining a class basis, unlike liberal theories which reject or dismiss class as an outmoded concept).

The concept of auto-valorization offered an important theoretical tool for understanding the growing manifestations of creative alternatives that were becoming increasingly important, especially for younger people in the late 1960s and early 1970s (Cleaver, 1992). Such manifestations included:

> the creative use of times, spaces and resources liberated from the control of Italian and multinational capital uses such as the proliferation of "free radio stations" or the widespread development of women's spaces which, along with many other self-managed projects, helped constitute what many came to call "the counter-culture." (Cleaver 1992, 129)

The tendency of capitalism to expand its valorization throughout the social factory initiates not only wider refusals, but also encourages a proliferation or growth in the number and diversity of self-valorizing projects to confront capital in the spaces opened by those refusals (Cleaver 1992, 131). This includes, crucially, new forms of social care or socialized (beyond the state) forms of welfare. The emphasis is shifted creatively and energetically from the value sought by capital to the values held by the subjugated.

> Where Marx's concept of valorisation draws our attention to the complex sequence of relationships through which capitalism renews itself as a social system of endlessly imposed work, so the concept of self-valorisation draws our attention *through* the complexity of our refusal of valorisation to our efforts to elaborate alternative autonomous projects which constitute the only possible source of a self-constituting alternative to capitalism. (Cleaver 1992, 131)

There are striking similarities between autonomist Marxist writings on self-valorization and anarchist writings on mutual aid and affinity. The types of concrete, actually-existing mutual aid activities initiated or supported by anarchists certainly embody the notion of self-valorization and the self-constitution of alternative modes of living, as discussed by Cleaver (1992). These are autonomous self-valorizing activities which, as discussed again by autonomists, are confronted by capitalist attempts at disvalorization. For anarchists, mutual aid, which makes up most of the survival mechanisms for the subjugated, serves as the basis for alternatives to capitalism. It is the basis of a new commons, a communism (see Shantz 2013). Mutual aid makes up its own transitional program. As Cleaver suggests:

> Negri's critique of traditional Marxist concepts of the "transition" from capitalism to communism, in which he argues that the only meaningful transition can occur through a development of self-valorising activities which negates capitalist command, makes clear that the concept of self-valorisation designates the existing ground of an emerging post-capitalism. (1992, 132)

Commonists try to avoid a productivist vision of life, emphasizing the great diversity of ways in which human life might be realized. Commonists again share common ground with anarchists and autonomist Marxists in arguing that the only way that work can be an interesting mode of self-realization for people is "through its subordination to the rest of life, the exact opposite of capitalism" (Cleaver 1992, 143, n. 59). And the socialized character of caring labor is restored as a human priority over and above the collectivized work of producing surplus value for capital.

SOCIALIZED WORK TO SOCIALIZED WELFARE

FOR MARX, THE PRINCIPLE ALIENATION of capitalism is the dominance of the thing (commodity, dead labor, death) over life. Today, in the context of precarious capitalism, the problem of life itself is at the center of debates, particularly since welfare, having been realized, has been defeated (Negri 2008, 208). Well, a particular form of welfare, statist welfare managed through the auspices of the Planner States, has been defeated. But another form arising from within the social sphere itself emerges, still uncertain, still insufficient. According to Negri, "Welfare represented an intervention of the state in life; at a certain point it was pulled apart by neoliberalism but also by its bureaucratic urges" (2008, 208). People want the state out of their lives (but do not want withdrawal of its social provisions in the vicious, demeaning, mean-spirited way undertaken by neoliberal regimes). For Negri, with regard to state provided welfare, "It had experienced a type of refusal by the people" (2008, 208). As Negri argues, "In short, the end of welfare wasn't due only to the defeat of the working class, but also to the exhaustion and the corruption of the bureaucratic agencies of the working class and the State" (2008, 208).

Crucially, the end of the welfare state affirmed a space of common autonomy. It left a great space "in the social autonomy of the multitude for the reconstruction of the common" (Negri 2008, 208). Yet when confronted by this opportunity or space, the organizations of the Left do not know how to proceed. For Negri, "The materiality of life, the freedom of passion, will not be dominated by anyone" (2008, 206). The new uprisings assert this desire not to be governed, not to be ruled, not to be dominated. And their refusal of domination extends not only against states and capital but against the traditional parties of the Left as well.

Socialized Welfare and Socialism?

Human survival has always depended on mutual aid, sociality, and care. Thus care is at the heart of socialized (collective) welfare and is the basis for the individual's life. There is, despite Thatcher's claim, and counter to it, no individual, no complete autonomy. Resistance is founded as a commons on the basis of affinity and affection. Mutual aid, which anarchists have always posed as the basis of resistance, forms relations of common struggle. Against the Crisis State discourses of security and risk, the new affinity groupings assert practices of communal care and socialized welfare. They pose a commons of care. This includes enhancing the status, as Lorey (2015, 91) puts it, of care activities like sex work, which have traditionally made much of the Left uncomfortable.

We have commonality in precarity. And rather than running from each other to seek our own individual capitalist market protection, we are called to care for one another in our shared and acknowledged vulnerability. This too disrupts traditional capitalist separations between production and reproduction. Capitalist production in pursuit of surplus value has always drained away time and energy for care relations and activities. The time and labor used up producing surplus value leaves one too tired or unable to take time to care for one's communities after the capitalist work day is done. That extends again conditions of precarity as waged workers hold or seek multiple jobs or have extra time taken in travel to and from the job(s). Care in mutual aid brings production and reproduction together again.

This is the basis for what some of us refer to as commonism. In commonism we create in common our collective futures. Mutual aid and commons of care are positioned against police forms of security based on threatening Others and the production of phobic identities (Ramadan and Shantz 2016).

Socialized Work to Socialized Welfare

The modes of production under Crisis State-managed post-Fordist frameworks extend beyond traditional forms of labor to encompass a range of life activities. Theorists of this socialized labor focus on communicative, cognitive, affective capacities and their flexible utilization. Thinking, speaking, feeling. This socialized work incorporates, and exploits, the whole personality rather than specific labor-related tasks of Fordist production models. Notably, this socialized production overflows the spaces and times of waged labor (Lorey 2015, 75). It is labor without end.

This is an interlocking of production with sociality in which both labor and social life are rendered quite precarious (Lorey 2015, 75). Labor as service work incorporates communication and affect (sympathy, empathy, etc.). This labor brings the whole person into the capitalist process of production (Lorey 2015, 83). And, of fundamental significance, the capitalist process of production now circulates socially. And subjectivities and socialities emerge in this process of production (Lorey 2015, 84).

Socialized work blurs the lines between private and public. New public spheres emerge and production becomes social. All human experiences are made part of the process of production. The hegemonic form of labor consumes the whole person, rather than specific, limited acts. It is affective, based on forms of sociality (care, communication, etc.). This is why questions of self-governance and subjectivity in relation to insecurity become important. But also why forms of socialized work become key.

On the one hand, self-governance serves to render people governable or even servile, as Heidi Rimke (2003) has discussed. The crisis-driven dismantling of collective welfare systems (not only statist ones) is coupled with a market-valorizing push to privatize (and individualize) welfare and risk management. As Lorey suggests:

> The new quality of insecurity arises not least through the erosion of workers' rights, the restructuring of social, health and educational systems, all the way through to the self-responsible prevention of illness and the loss of wages and pensions. Consequently, a neoliberal individualized self-government and self-responsibility is partly confronted with existential precariousness in a new way. (2015, 89)

The notion that a better life is a matter of individual responsibility, rather than communal action is illusory. Yet, under crisis conditions, people are set in competition with others to secure themselves and their social sphere. This then further undercuts communal action and reinforces individualist approaches in a form of state-managed social Darwinism.

Life is entirely interwoven with politics. At the end of the day, the question is one of welfare. Politics (under neoliberalism) has wanted to withdraw from the things of life, because capitalists insinuated the suspicion that it lacked the money to manage the things of life (thus austerity and so forth) (Negri 2008, 207).

A baby is, for Negri, the beginning of the common "because it sets the whole society to work around it. The foundling has always been a very beautiful figure from this point of view" (2008, 207). This is an embodiment of shared labor in the creation and sustenance, the flourishing of life. Under capitalism, though, even this is imperiled as the labor of child care becomes privatized and undersupported. And typically on gendered lines of domination.

This too speaks to the distinction between self-valorization and capitalist valorization. Negri argues, "Money that we invest in life stays in the body of the children we make" (2008, 207).

Yet under capitalist relations this becomes uncertain, a point of struggle.

Negri has argued that the movements of the socialized worker would break with the defensive attitude to restructuring to challenge the Crisis State's managerial control of society (see Dyer-Witheford 1999, 83). Movements of the socialized worker "are informed by an ethic that 'emphasises the connections of social labour and highlights the importance of social cooperation,' and express, in a diffuse but unmistakable form, an aspiration that 'cooperative production can be led from the base, the globality of the post-industrial economy can be assumed by social subjects'" (Dyer-Witheford 1999, 83). Key aspects of the movements of the socialized worker include the emphasis on autonomy and the construction of alternative social structures (Hardt 1996)

The new subjectivities emerging from the transition to post-Fordism, "far from passively accepting the terrain of productive flexibility, appropriated the social terrain as a space of struggle and self-valorization" (Vercellone 1996, 84). And they raise strategies and tactics based on their own needs rather than pre-given notions of comportment. As Michael Hardt suggests:

> Self-valorization was a principal concept that circulated in the movements, referring to social forms and structures of value that were relatively autonomous from and posed an effective alternative to capitalist circuits of valorization. Self-valorization was thought of as the building block for constructing a new form of sociality, a new society. (Hardt 1996, 3)

Autonomists refer to these radical and participatory forms of democracy which thrive "outside the power of the State and its mechanisms of representation" as a constituent power, "a free association of constitutive social forces" (Hardt 1996, 5–6). The socialized care within movements poses both a defensive and a constructive aspect. As Hardt suggests, "Self-valorization is one way of understanding the circuits that constitute an alternative sociality, autonomous from the control of the State or capital"

(1996, 6). These movements are engaged in projects to develop democratic and autonomous communities/social relations beyond political representation and hierarchy.

Some theorists have sought to identify social forms of welfare that might constitute alternative networks outside of state control (Hardt 1996; see Vercellone 1996 and Del Re 1996). For radical political theorists in Italy, the experiences of the social movements "show the possibilities of alternative forms of welfare in which systems of aid and socialization are separated from State control and situated instead in autonomous social networks. These alternative experiments may show how systems of social welfare will survive the crisis of the Welfare State" (Vercellone 1996, 81).

In these struggles exists the possibility of alternative forms of welfare "based on autonomous self-management and social solidarity outside of State control" (Vercellone 1996, 96). As Del Re suggests, part of the new parameters for change includes "the proposal to go beyond welfare by taking as our goal the improvement of the quality of life, starting from the reorganization of the time of our lives" (1996, 110). I agree with Hardt's assertion that the first and primary tasks of political theory are "to identify, affirm, and further the existing instances of social power that allude to a new alternative society, a coming community" (1996, 7). I also agree with Hardt that radical Italian theorists are rights in "continually proposing the impossible as if it were the only reasonable option" (1996, 7). As he suggests: "It is our task to translate this revolutionary potential, to make the impossible real in our own contexts" (Hardt 1996, 7). Illuminati suggests that in the contemporary context "politics has spread out into spheres from which it has traditionally been excluded and where, hence, it has to be reinterpreted" (1996, 167). There is no replaying of the politics outside of the new forms of precarity and socialized work in a way that can challenge systems of exploitation, oppression, and repression.

The context of constituent power, the power that disintegrates constituted power, "is impoverished experience, reduced to the nakedness of the rules and confronted by the powers of the abstract, while its conflictual articulation requires a structure that is nonrepresentative and does not homologize citizenship" (Illuminati 1996, 173). The structure of action of constituent power "requires a plurality of distinct unities, agents, and reflections, and discards both the solipsism of 'private languages' and the internal dialectic of the will, along with the tendency of a social or institutional representation to fuse subjectivities together" (Illuminati 1996, 173). This refers specifically to structures of a party in which previous socialists have sought the space for a re/combination of the diverse forces of the exploited and oppressed.

The "S" Words: Socialized Work and ... Socialism?

For many social commentators the new forms of communications, affective labor, and socialized welfare hold out particular promise for social change and alternatives to capitalist relations. As Negri explains, "I mean to say only that I believe that the inventors of new modes of communicative living are much more socialist than capitalist, much more tied to a concept of solidarity than to that of profit" (2008, 23). Industrialism and totalitarianism cannot exist together because the population cannot be forced to work in the form of slaves any longer (Negri 2008, 201). Liberation is the appropriation of cognitive capital, taking the instruments of communication and managing them positively, socially. There is not postmodern production without freedom.

One of the real problems of socialism was a problem of communication. The management of needs was too bureaucratic, centralized, and authoritarian. More agile, diffuse management, and transmission of information might have allowed for more simplification of the bureaucratic structure without information being made to pass through a centralized command structure (Negri 2008, 23).

For Negri, the term *socialism* still has political space. It will continue to make the rounds on the margins of contemporary ideology (as the survivors of Bonapartism are still around) (Negri 2008). For Negri, categories like socialism, fascism, Stalinism, or totalitarianism are too generic to add much to the understanding of historical reality. It is more interesting to look at how the struggle between poor and rich, proletarian and bourgeois invests and qualifies these concepts (2008).

Negri argues that, contrary to the history of the Church, communism is free from its Constantine (from Stalinism), from the taste of power (2008, 26). Communism is more extensive, including quite diverse cultural contexts such as feminism, postcolonial studies, informational cultures. It is re-emerging in its libertarian or anarchistic forms, which had been marginalized, silenced, obscured with the rise of the statist forms since the Russian Revolution.

New understandings are emerging, returning notions of social care and the commons to the forefront. Communism is being rethought as the "radical modification of subjects forced to work" and as "the construction of the 'common,' as in the *common* capacity to produce and reproduce the social in freedom" (Negri 2008, 260). This is an expression of what I have termed *commonism* (Shantz 2013). For Negri, "Inside it is an ideal of communism and of radical egalitarianism that no longer has any type of qualification, for example, of an anarcho-individualistic type" (2008, 27). In the movements against austerity a new type of social (non)representation emerges beyond the remnants of a defeated extraparliamentary Left (as exist in sectarian factions, mini-Maoisms, Trotskyist cults, and others replaying the road of 1917 in their study groups).

It is a great transition, in which a separated multitude emerges and recomposes politically and socially (Negri 2008, 94). It is organized efficaciously, not technologically — in networks of affection or affinity rather than the party. Groupings have tried to express a coherent mass power of resistance and defense. The movements destabilize the practices of power (Negri 2008, 96). Leading groups face the current challenge of not distracting the multitude from going toward the possibility of uprising nor of organizing it. There is a conundrum of how to keep afloat a multitudinous mass (Negri 2008). According to Negri, "We don't know what we are doing as far as demonstrations are concerned, and thus we entrust ourselves to a pragmatic, not theoretical, way of acting" (Negri 2008, 101). And this has a nice habit of avoiding old habits and breaking with previous prejudices.

I have termed the new forms of mobilization and social care *commonism*. This suggests a communism outside hierarchal forms and based on mutual aid and distributed engagement. This has implications for an imminent commons against capitalism.

Socialized work and communal cooperation, mutual aid, split from the production relations of crisis capitalism. Many analysts have looked to Paolo Virno's notion of exodus in explaining this. For Virno this cooperative sociality occurs at a distance from sovereignty, away from the state (2004). This exodus is, for Virno, a mass defection from the state that articulates "a non-state run public sphere" or what can be called socialized welfare (Virno 2004, 68). This is a refusal of capitalist valorization of social life and the trying of new forms of life, experimenting with the uncontrollable. It is a movement of scission in the sense of the term offered by revolutionary syndicalist Georges Sorel. This is a constituent power. It is a recomposition of relations of affinities.

Notably Negri has shifted his language somewhat in *Goodbye Mr. Socialism*. Rather than speaking of the general intellect, as some autonomist theorists have preferred and is a key concept in Negri's own recent works on Empire, he speaks of the commons. Among other things, this shift re-emphasizes the embodied character of intellect moving beyond the tendency toward a dualist confusion regarding cognitive labor. It also emphasizes the connection, at the center for Negri, between the crucial components of the global precariat (displaced migrant manual labor and the precarious technological classes).

Negri is convinced that a radical democracy provides today "the arms of liberation" for people of various countries (2008, 124). This is not a neoconservative vision of democracy as an American export. Such a vision, with its forms of power and reproduction of order, "means the maintenance of a class structure and of indecent exploitation that doesn't improve the current situation" (2008, 124). For Negri, "There exists, instead, another terrain, that of real and absolute democracy, on which we should fight without timidity or hesitations" (2008, 126). When Negri speaks of solidarity, he means "the articulation of subjectivity within the common" (2008, 28). This is not a centralized subsuming of identity. It is more than an articulation of disparate subject positions. And the common is not pregiven or preordained. It is expressed in the struggles against crisis.

No Guarantees

There are no guarantees, however, that crisis and precarity will give rise to resistance or prove real challenges to states and capital, let alone present alternative modes of living. While there are compelling examples of resistance and forms of solidarity-based alternatives, these have not yet endangered the existing social order.

Rather, it appears that large sections of populations in North America and Europe have conformed to conditions of crisis and austerity, have come to terms with them. And these allowances have been made by people of different statuses and for distinct reasons.

In part it relates to the fear of precarity itself — a result of the privatization of insecurity and the fear of falling out or being left behind. Part of it is a related fear that one can be readily replaced — by someone even more precarious, more in crisis, more alone, and more ready to conform.

The increase of policing and repression that has always accompanied neoliberal governance, and cannot be overlooked by a focus on socialization, serves these purposes well. Under Crisis State practices social welfare occurs in a frame of police and military security. Thus, it involves increases in surveillance, monitoring, control. To be precarious is also to be brought more fully within regimes of regulation.

Organization

The unresolved problem remains, as ever it is, the question of organization. This is the question of politics itself. The exhilaration of risings overshadows the essential, if tedious, work of building infrastructures. Of digging in for the long haul and preparing resources for a sustained struggle out of the crisis states of today. Some hip anarchists like to proclaim that such politics are "boring as fuck." And indeed building infrastructures of resistance can, like anything, have tedious, even banal, moments. But even more boring than this work is repeatedly losing.

And really, it is rather strange that the acts of building resources, sharing experiences, developing longer-term provisions to sustain communities in struggle would ever be viewed as boring. As opposed to what? Pursuing self-satisfied, and exclusionary, subcultures? Building infrastructures of resistance is the shared capacity for care. It is the arming of joy. This is the excitement of living and learning together.

On the question of such organizing beyond the state Badiou suggests, "For two centuries now the sole political problem has been this: How are we to make the inventions of movement communism endure?" (2012, 112).

The bulk of working people, the precarious, have minimal or no control over essential matters affecting their lives. They have no real voice in the decisions that impact their life chances and realities, from the distribution of community resources to the care of their neighbors to the condition of their environment (social and natural). The majority are present in the world but absent from decisions about it (Badiou 2012, 55–57). The recent movements, uprisings, suggest that those who are absent, excluded from decisions, are insisting on deciding — for themselves.

What in politics is called organization is "the labour of the new truth" (Badiou 2012, 63). The movements must secure sites where they can decide their own destiny.

In the current continuity of war one loses the capacity to be always present and active (Negri 2008, 123). This is a threat always faced by movements, and the well-known problems of "burnout" and demoralization and drift are real (and all too human). The state with its institutions does not face such threats in any way analogous to the movements. As Negri notes, "But this is part of that temporal asymmetry that power uses when faced by the power of the movements, in order to extinguish them in the long run when it doesn't manage to defeat them on the ground immediately" (2008, 123). This is one of the pressing reasons that infrastructures of resistance are of such critical importance to movements. They offer temporal and spatial supports beyond the individuals directly involved at any given point or time (Shantz 2010).

On organization, Badiou suggests, "I maintain that the time of organization, the time of construction of an empirical duration of the Idea in its post-riot stage, is crucial. Otherwise, we end up thinking that the state must endlessly retain a monopoly on the definition of political time" (2012, 90).

This is a point that insurrectionists often overlook. The delirious joy of insurrection, or even simply riots, provides a perhaps necessary release for direct participants and maybe some hopeful observers. But it does not do nearly enough to change the balance of power and/or conditions of struggle. There is too much of the safety valve in riots and insurrections, a point conservative sociologists like Durkheim have remarked upon and lauded (as beneficial for the longer-term maintenance of the status quo).

REFERENCES

Aufheben. 1998. "The Politics of Anti-Road Struggle and the Struggles of Anti-Road Politics: The Case of the No M11 Link Road Campaign." In *DiY Culture: Party and Protest in Nineties Britain,* George McKay, ed. London: Verso, 100–128.

Aviram, Hadar. 2015. *Cheap on Crime: Recession-Era Politics and the Transformation of American Punishment.* Berkeley: University of California Press.

Badiou, Alain. 2012. *The Rebirth of History: Times of Riots and Uprisings.* London: Verso.

Butler, Judith. 2015. "Foreword." *State of Insecurity: Government of the Precarious.* London: Verso, vii–xi.

Cleaver, Harry. 1992. "The Inversion of Perspective in Marxian Theory: From Valorisation to Self-Valorisation." In *Open Marxism Volume II: Theory and Practice,* Werner Bonefield, Richard Gunn, and Kosmas Psychopedis, eds. London: Pluto, 106–144.

Del Re, Alisa. 1996. "Women and Welfare: Where is Jocasta?" In *Radical Thought in Italy: A Potential Politics,* Paolo Virno and Michael Hardt, eds. Minneapolis: University of Minnesota Press, 99–113.

Dyer-Witheford, Nick. 1999. *Cyber-Marx: Cycles and Circuits of Struggle in High-Technology Capitalism.* Urbana and Chicago: University of Illinois Press.

Elder, Larry. 2012. *Dear Father, Dear Son: Two Lives...Eight Hours.* Medford, OR: WND Books.

———. 2001. *Ten Things You Can't Say in America.* New York: St. Martin's.

Hardt, Michael. 1996. "Introduction: Laboratory Italy." In *Radical Thought in Italy: A Potential Politics,* Paolo Virno and Michael Hardt, eds. Minneapolis: University of Minnesota Press, 1–10.

Illuminati, Augusto. 1996. "Unrepresentable Citizenship." In *Radical Thought in Italy: A Potential Politics,* Paolo Virno and Michael Hardt, eds. Minneapolis, MN: University of Minnesota Press, 167–188.

Leonhardt, David. 2010. "A Progressive Agenda to Remake Washington." *New York Times* May 21. http://www.nytimes.com/2010/05/22/business/economy/22leonhardt.html.

Lorey, Isabell. 2015. *State of Insecurity: Government of the Precarious.* London: Verso.

McKay, George. 1998. "DiY Culture: Notes Towards an Intro." In *DiY Culture: Party and Protest in Nineties Britain,* George McKay, ed. London: Verso, 1–53.

Moran, Dominique. 2015. *Carceral Geography: Spaces and Practices of Incarceration.* Farnham, Surrey: Ashgate.

Moynihan, Daniel Patrick. 1986. *Family and Nation.* New York: Harcourt.

Noble, Richard E. n.d. "The National Debt with a Noble Solution." http://www.federalbudget.com/noble.html.

Ramadan, Hisham and Jeff Shantz. 2016. *Manufacturing Phobias.* Toronto: University of Toronto Press.

Seitz-Wald, Alex. 2011. "10 Things Conservatives don't want you to Know about Ronald Reagan." *Think Progress* Feb. 5. http://thinkprogress.org/politics/2011/02/05/142288/reagan-centennial/.

Shantz, Jeff. 2013. *Commonist Tendencies: Mutual Aid beyond Communism.* Brooklyn, NY: punctum books.

———. 2012. *Crime, Punishment, Power: Sociological Explanations.* Dubuque, IA: Kendall Hunt.

———. 2010. *Constructive Anarchy: Building Infrastructures of Resistance.* Farnham, Surrey: Ashgate.

Spicer, Myles. 2012. "It's Time for a Ronald Reagan Reality Check." *Daily KOS* Jan. 11. http://www.dailykos.com/story/2012/01/11/1053759/-It-s-time-for-a-Ronald-Reagan-reality-check.

Vercellone, Carlo. 1996. "The Anomaly and Exemplariness of the Italian Welfare State." In *Radical Thought in Italy: A Po-*

tential Politics, Paolo Virno and Michael Hardt, eds. Minneapolis: University of Minnesota Press, 80–95.

Virno, Paolo. 2004. *A Grammar of the Multitude: For an Analysis of Contemporary Forms of Life.* Los Angeles and New York: Semiotext(e).

Wilson, William Julius. 2010. *More than Just Race: Being Black and Poor in the Inner City.* New York: W.W. Norton

———. 1997. *When Work Disappears: The World of the New Urban Poor.* New York: Vintage.

———. 1993. *The Declining Significance of Race.* Chicago, IL: University of Chicago Press.

www.ingramcontent.com/pod-product-compliance
Lightning Source LLC
Chambersburg PA
CBHW071031280326
41935CB00011B/1539